Cricut for Beginners

The Ultimate Guide to Mastering Cricut Machines With Quick and Easy, Practical Examples to Realize Your Ideas and Projects

Paul S. Leland

Tîrgu Neamţ, 2021

ISBN 978-973-0-35418-8

Table of Contents

Preface

Do you enjoy making crafts? There's nothing more satisfying than a DIY project that gives you the end result exactly as you need it!

Fully understanding how to use any DIY arts and crafts project's primary tool is the key to success in your creation.

The Cricut machine is your first choice among clipping machines, whether you're into making T-shirts, pillow cover, or hammocks.

This book is a beginner's guide for all DIY lovers who have no idea what a Cricut machine is. It is your go-to guide for all-things Cricut.

Read on to learn more about an innovative machinery that allows people to make projects and build interesting objects.

Introduction

Smart-cutting is an invention of the future! With the dawn of this new futuristic era, it is hard not to be surprised at the technological world's advancements. Smart-cutting tools and machinery are one of these unique and innovative ideas that have the potential to change the world. Smart-cutting refers to cutting materials and fabrics electronically with the help of precision machining tech. In the world of modern manufacturing, smart-cutting tools play an incredibly important role. They allow the user to position and cut with high accuracy and consistency.

The smart-cutting process that these tools and machines use is proactive. They use ultra-precision and micro-machining technologies and keep the surface roughness at a nanometre scale and the features at a micrometer level. It provides enhanced functionality and performance, hence paving the way for the future of electronic cutting.

The Cricut is a premium smart-cutting tool. Its exceptional features and innovative and sleek designs allow it to be one of the most popular and widely used smart-cutting machine. The cutting-edge technology integrated into the Cricut construction enables you to perform even the most high-intensity cutting projects with ease and convenience. From jewelry and décor to 3-D art and vinyl crafts, the Cricut allows you to seamlessly part and create anything you want. Using the Cricut without knowing everything about it can be a bit difficult. This book tells you everything you need to know about the Cricut– from its components and parts to its various uses and purposes. Go on and read to find out everything you need to know to become an expert at using Cricut.

Chapter 1: What is a Cricut Machine?

Smart-cutting allows one to carve and cut out pieces of vinyl, cardboard, fabrics, leather, and even wood. The Cricut is an all-powerful smart-cutting tool that was designed to make life easier for craftsmen and DIY-creators. Whether you want to build a wooden toy for your children or cut out a few stickers for hard surfaces, this innovative cutting machine has got you covered.

The Cricut is one of the best smart-cutting tools in the market. It offers a ton of features and high-performance at low costs. It is also an easy-to-use machine, and the software that comes with it is quite simple to learn. Its blades are precise, and the Cricut image library is gigantic. There is absolutely nothing you can't do with a Cricut. Using advanced tools and technology, the Cricut enables you to work on any cutting-related project you want. This is a useful tool to own in today's time, especially if you or your children are interested in making arts-and-crafts'projects.

One thing that the Cricut can be used for is the growingly-popular 'cut-out' stickers. These 3-D stickers are created using smart-cutting tools and then sold for reasonable prices all over the world. You can make personally designed and customized cut-out stickers for your laptops, notebooks, and even cars with your Cricut.

With the latest Cricut machines, you can construct virtually any project with intricate details and superior precision. Halloween décor like spider webs, artificial pumpkins, and 3-D modelled ghost figurines, as well as Christmas decoration items like snow-flakes and Christmas tree models. The new Cricut machines can cut through tough fabrics and thick materials, making it easy to create something out of anything at all.

Cricut Pens can also be used to create hand-made cards and other projects. You can choose from over 350 fonts or incorporate a font from your computer for no cost. All you have to do is sit back and watch the Cricut work its magic. Cricut machines create flawless fold lines and cards, as well as envelopes, boxes, and pinwheels. Working on 3-D crafts has never been easier! Cricuts are known for their accuracy and high-precision. Their ability to cut through hundreds of materials is unparalleled. Tough and sturdy materials like matboards and basswood can easily be parted by the innovative smart-cutting tools that the Cricut implements.

Cricut's Rotary Blades will enable you to work on high-end sewing projects by seamlessly cutting through all kinds of fabric with ease. Alternatively, you can use Knife Blades to cut denser materials with added depth and dimension. You can switch between their various specialty tips to score, engrave, deboss, or perform other material functions as per your choice.

With the Cricut, making your designs and cutting them out is as simple as pressing a few buttons to print and cut. Cricut's library offers over 60,000 images filled with inspiration and creativity. 3,000 projects are also readily available for you to kick start your creative streak all at once. Simply choose the images you like and allow your Cricut device to cut the pictures and patterns in unique ways. A collection of 50,000 printable images and over 900 patterns are present for you to pick from in the design software that corresponds to the smart-cutting machine: Design Space. You can also choose to upload your images to cut and do projects with.

Cricut's most desirable and exciting feature is its cutting speed. New Cricut machine models offer a 'Fast Mode' that allows the user to cut up to two times faster than any average cutting machine! Writing on vinyl and cardboard surfaces is also made extremely smooth with this attractive feature.

From delicate items like paper to thick and dense materials like leather, the Cricut is well-equipped to deal with all. It offers a 'Smart Set' dial, along with the option to select a custom material in Design Space software, offering the user a variety of different material settings at their fingertips. With the Cricut smart-cutting machine, you can cut over a hundred other materials and products.

While Design Space may sound like a technological complexity, in truth, the app is incredibly user-friendly and straightforward. Its easy-to-learn interface makes it popular amongst users of all age groups. Think of this app as a blank page waiting to be filled with your creative and exciting ideas. Anything is possible here! From Cricut starters to expert and specialized artisans, the Design Space app is enough to accommodate everyone. It's a cloud-based design app that is free for all to use and create, offering limitless creative possibilities. This robust design app is second to none.

The best part about working with Cricuts and Design Space is that you can use it on multiple platforms since it is a cloud-based application. Design Space is compatible with Windows, Android, and iOS. Whether you are on your phone, laptop, or computer—when creative inspiration strikes, you know just what to do! All you have to do is open your app and get started. Design Space allows you to save your projects and work on them whenever you want. You can also download projects on your devices to use offline, even without access to the Internet. You don't have to wait for anything!

Design Space's intuitive and simple layout, along with the numerous tutorials and instructions, makes it a very straightforward and non-complex app. All you need to do is design, refine, and then cut out your project. With Design Space, you can start bringing your artistic ideas to life right away! Another amazing benefit that Design Space offers is allowing the users to upload their images, including drawings, fonts, photos, and patterns. You can create personalized projects for yourself and your family and friends with just a few clicks.

For beginners in the world of DIY arts-and-crafts, the Cricut is the perfect tool. Its superb usability and premium image collection allows one to create ready-to-make projects from the Cricut library. Cricut also offers superior customer support in case you run into any trouble. Because of its smooth-cutting abilities, thousands of artists and crafters worldwide are using this brilliant cutting device. Not only is the Cricut one of the fastest smart-cutting machines in the market, but it is also one of the quietest. While cutting, one of the most significant issues you may face is that the device is too noisy, and others around you, including yourself, are being disturbed. Loud noises disrupt the creative process in dangerous ways. Once an idea slips out of your mind, it isn't easy to gather the motivation to work on it again. Choosing to work with Cricut means that your creative process remains as smooth as possible. With the Cricut, you will never run into any problems, especially noise-related ones.

Buying a Cricut is an incredible option if you are looking for smart-cutting devices on a budget. Not only are they super inexpensive, but the brand also offers special discounts and deals. During the sale season, you might be able to purchase multiple accessories along with the Cricut machine itself. Extra blades and cutting mats are always needed! And if you ever want to upgrade to a newer machine, the Cricut resale values are incredibly high and established.

Cricuts are brilliant tools for smart-cutting, for beginners and experts alike. They offer you the creative freedom to make anything you can imagine, from sewing and paper projects to vinyl decals and leather crafts. You can even create balsa and wood models with the miraculous Cricut cutting machine. It offers endless, possibly! With an extended suite of various tools and powerful blades, the Cricut is virtually undefeatable when it comes to cutting. Its pens and scoring tools are also one of a kind. You will grow as you learn, with your artistic abilities expanding and creative ideas increasing.

A new and innovative component that Cricut has introduced is the latest Rotary Blade in their machines. Its smooth gliding and rolling actions are unrivaled by competitors. This blade can cut through anything! The Cricut's Rotary Blade has made accuracy and precision an ultimate priority. It also cuts through the fabric and other materials at incredibly fast speeds. The Cricut machine simplifies working with cloth and textile materials as well. It offers various digital sewing patterns that allow the user to make sewing and quilting projects with comfort and convenience. The Cricut devices cuts and marks all the pieces for you, making sewing a simpler experience than ever before. The newer generation finds it hard to be interested in the previous generation's activities. Still, with the Cricut and its endless sewing projects' availability, now you and your grandparents (or grandchildren) can bond over this fun and exciting activity! Showcase your artistic talents for everyone to see.

The Design Space app allows you to view and edit your projects as you go along. You can virtually create anything and bring it to life with the wondrous Cricut technology. Whether you are a starter or a professional, the Design Space app will quickly become your go-to place to begin creating arts and crafts for any purpose. Upload your images and favorite fonts on to the software and cut them smoothly with the new Cricut at your convenience! One of the best features that the Cricut offers is its thoughtful details. Cricut was designed to make creating arts and crafts easier for any artist. It provides a docking slot, which is quite useful and allows one to keep their phone or tablet as you work. You can also charge your device using a suitable USB port, which allows for quick and easy charging.

Cricut's Design App is compatible with an array of different devices and operating systems. It functions perfectly well on macOS, as well as Windows and Android smartphones. A Cricut machine applies about 4 kg of force on the material, which allows for perfectly well-cut results. The latest Cricut devices embody an exciting feature is the extra storage, which is built-in to keep the accessories and tools needed for the smart-cutting process on hand and organized. If you are a professional designer, buying a Cricut to assist you with your design requirements and needs is the way to go. It can cut through hundreds of materials, from even the most delicate fabric to strong and sturdy wooden boards. For thicker materials (up to 2.4 mm), you can always separately purchase a Knife Blade. These blades can cut through thick fabrics and clothing seamlessly and without any faults. The Rotary Blade that comes with the Cricut can cut through any material without a backer. Making cloth projects has never been this easy!

Another one of the Cricut's useful accessories is the Scoring Wheel, which can cut razor-sharp creases in cardboards, poster boards, and other dense materials. The Scoring Wheel is also sold separately but is available at low and affordable costs. Another accessory that you can purchase with the Cricut is the Washable Fabric Pen. This item marks pattern pieces that need to be cut by the Cricut and then sewn together by hand or machine. As the name suggests, this pen is easily washable and can be used multiple times. Cricuts have an adaptive tool system. They are said to learn with you as you advance your projects and higher tier ones.

Cricuts follow your journey from a beginner to a professional as your design companions. They can also be connected via wireless Bluetooth technology to your phones, computers, and laptops. No matter which material you are trying to cut or carve, your Cricut machine will always be there to help you.

Cricuts come equipped with a Rotary Blade and a Premium Fine-Point Blade. They also come with a Fine Point Pen in black, a FabricGrip Mat (12-by-12 inches), a LightGrip Mat (also 12-by-12 inches), and a USB cable. A welcome book is included along with a power adapter and a free trial membership to Cricut Access. You receive 50 ready-to-make projects, which include 25 different sewing patterns for sewing and quilting projects. You also receive the materials for a practice project, so you can start to learn how to work with Cricut with ease and simplicity.

Different Models of the Cricut Machine

Currently, there are three Cricut machines available in the market. All of them have their unique features and functions. They are as follows:

The Cricut Joy

The Cricut Joy is the latest release in the Cricut family. This impeccable device is relatively small but can cut and draw a wide variety of items and materials. Its special feature is that this smart-cutting tool can cut through materials like vinyl and iron-on even without a mat!

The Cricut Maker

This member of the Cricut family is one of the most powerful smart-cutting machines in the world. It allows one to cut with ten times more strength than the other Cricut devices. With the Cricut Maker, you can not only cut and draw, but you can also deboss and score any material you wish!

The Cricut Explore

The Cricut Explore is the most common Cricut out there. There are three models in the Cricut Explore line of smart-cutting machines, and although they can all cut the same material, they all have different features. The Cricut Explore One and the Cricut Explore Air were the original machines introduced by Cricut. Cricut no longer sells these devices, but you can certainly buy them used at great prices. The Cricut Explore Air 2 has the same features as the Explore Air, including cutting, scoring, printing, and drawing, but is up to two times faster than the prior device. Its speedy cutting makes it a good contender for smart-cutting devices on a budget.

Chapter 2: What Can You Do with a Cricut Machine?

Now that we have established and learned about what a Cricut is, it is time to look at what a Cricut machine can do. All kinds of artists and designers use Cricuts; beginners, and pros. They allow you to create beautiful crafts and projects with different materials– fabric, leather, cardboard, and wood. With the right Cricut machine, you can even emboss, deboss, draw on, and cut any material you want. You can make 3-D projects, greeting cards, boxes, and quilts with a Cricut.

Even if you are simply an art lover, owning a Cricut can come in handy. You don't need to be a proficient artist to use this useful smart-cutting device. It's so simple to use that almost anyone can! All you need is a little bit of guidance, and that is what this book is for. Since the Cricut devices launch, people of all age groups have used these brilliant smart-cutting tools to perform hundreds of thousands of tasks.

There are many projects that you can make with a Cricut smart-cutting tool. A good part about using this brilliant machine is that it can easily carve through wood, such as balsa and basswood. You might need to buy a separate Knife Blade to cut through wood easily, but it is certainly a worthwhile purchase. With the additional Knife Blade, you can cut through wood as if it's made of wool! Cutting hard and sturdy materials has never been easier. The Knife Blade is designed to cut thick materials.

There are many projects that you can accomplish with a decent Cricut machine. Here is a list of a few.

Home Décor

Decorating your home can be quite a personal task. While some people may prefer to buy decoration pieces and wall paintings ready-made, other homeowners would instead add a personalized touch to their homes. If you are of the latter kind of people, here's some good news! Cricut machines can undoubtedly help you out with this.

Making decals for your windows and walls or designing baskets and spice bottles in your kitchen will add a homely touch to your décor. With a Cricut device, there are many crafty, trendy, colorful, and exciting décor ideas that you can implement! You can design wall hangings by etching on glass with the Cricut machine or cut out quotes in your favorite fonts to be framed and hung. These will bring warmth and comfort to your home space.

You can also create hanging planters with a Cricut! Hanging planters or baskets are used to hold hanging plants and are usually hung low from ceilings or rooftops. They look remarkable and add an element of gracefulness and elegance to your surroundings. With a Cricut cutting machine, you can cut out minimalistic hanging planters made of white paper or cardboard.

Your plants will look beautiful placed in these hand-made hanging planters, and you will feel more connected to them because of your efforts in building them a stunning home.

Using a Cricut smart-cutting device, you can also cut and design customized doormats for your home. Write whatever you wish in the font of your choice! You can also make DIY-mouse pads for your computer's mouse and other electronic accessories. You can make iron-on vinyl patches for your clothing or curtains and look fabulous! Mini-quilts and projects related to your favorite movies, TV shows, and books can be undertaken, resulting in a uniquely and entirely yours home. A popular item on the market is a Game of Thrones based bedside lamp, which is decorated with the quote 'Winter is Coming' and the show's symbols. It looks splendid! You can choose to decorate your lights in whichever way you please with a Cricut machine.

Etching on mirrors is an underrated design technique. You cannot only write or draw anything on mirrors with a brand-new Cricut machine, but you can also cut out drawings and patterns that you can adorn the mirrors of your house with. Mirrors look excellent with designs on them! Not to mention, this would make your mirror-selfies and photographs all the more enticing.

An exciting creation that you can create with a Cricut is a world map or a map of the country you reside in. That way, you can keep track of your trips and the places you want to travel to. You can use your Cricut to cut paper, corkscrew boards, or cardboards for these maps, and use different colored pins or thumb-tacks to identify the places you want to visit. You can also cut rough cloth like jute or burlap and attach it to create 3-D flowers and other items. They look quite heart-warming and bring about a comforting vibe to the place. Cutting out Hessian fabric with a Cricut machine can also make wall hangings and doormats of different shapes and sizes.

With the Cricut Infusible Ink technology, you can construct and transfer your designs onto a base material, like fabric or paper. This technology creates designs that are seamless and smooth, but they stay on the base material for years to come. The results of the Infusible Ink feature of the Cricut are mind-blowing! Their high-quality designs are breath-taking. With a Cricut device, you can use the Infusible Ink feature to create delightful customized coasters. These can be made in different colors, shapes, and sizes to fit the aesthetic of your home perfectly.

You can create customized statement pieces for every room in your house, as well as a wall hook set for your guests and visitors to hang their coats and jackets on. Buying a Cricut will give you several different ideas on how to set up your home perfectly. You can also make succulents and plants out of paper or other materials. They look regal in every setting! You can also create reusable stencils and photo frames with a Cricut by using it to cut wood or other sturdy materials. The items you make will have the advantage of being hand-made, and you will also save costs by creating them instead of buying them. Hand-made items bring a very comforting and homely feel to an area. They are unmatched!

These items can also make great gifts for your family, friends, and loved ones. You will be able to customize them to your loved ones' liking, and they will be touched to receive a gift personally created by you. It's a win-win!

Holiday Décor

Holidays consist of spending time with your loved ones filled with celebration, love, and warmth! What other way can you achieve that than by creating personalized décor and decoration pieces with them?

Birthdays

You can sit with your loved ones for birthdays and create paper pinwheels for décor or even for fun. You can also make things with felt, like plants, succulents, and wall-hangings. Felt is a perfect medium to work with, as it is easy to cut and draw on. You can choose the pattern of your choice and make virtually anything you want! You can also send people personalized gifts for their birthdays using your Cricut machine. Even if you're going to give them a store-bought gift, you can always choose to decorate the box or make personalized wrapping paper for your loved ones.

Christmas

For the Christmas holidays, there is a wide array of décor items that you can make! From a DIY-reindeer made of Papier-mâché (cut from a Cricut machine, of course) to baubles for your Christmas tree, anything is possible! These will add fun and colorful touches to your Christmas decorations. You and your family will enjoy spending time working with one another, too. Having movie-nights and opening gifts on the morning of Christmas is always fun, but it is also incredibly enjoyable to work and create with your loved ones, especially if you love arts andcrafts.

You can design and print banners and reindeer panels for your Christmas tree! Minimalistic designs are all the rage these days, and with a Cricut, you can create absolutely anything you like. You can also make wood ornaments for your tree, which add sentimental value to your décor. Use different materials to create textured designs will keep you occupied in a fun activity with your close friends and family. You can use various craft techniques like folding, cutting, and creasing, to create many of the most personalized decoration items for your favorite holiday. You can go through the designs available on Design Space and choose from there, or browse the web and pick out something you can do with everyone that looks fun and exciting. The possibilities are endless! You can also cut vinyl patches and designs with your Cricut and paste them on blank mugs or empty walls. You can fill up photo frames with a cut-out photo of your family. There is nothing you can't do with a Cricut. You can also decorate your Christmas stockings and design them with anything you like. You can add quotes or images on it, or even the symbols of your favorite football teams. Vinyl can also be pasted on the glass to provide delicate but beautiful designs. You can also cut out fabrics in different Christmas-themed shapes and sew them on pillows and cushions that are present for everyone to see.

Halloween

Halloween is the season for spooky décor! Since Cricut machines are great for carving, there is a lot that you can create for this season. From decorating your pumpkin to creating wooden signboards that lead to your house, Cricut devices were designed for this season. There are many scary and silly items that you can design with a Cricut that will fit in with the Halloween style.

Halloween is a season that requires intricate details and cuts on the décor. Spider webs, haunted houses, and delicate wreaths— all of these can be made with a fully functional Cricut cutting machine. You can design mugs and other pottery with cut-out drawings of pumpkins, skeletons, and ghosts. Halloween is the perfect occasion to showcase your artistic skills. You can try making spider web pinwheels. These are made with black-colored paper or cardboard and look marvelous. They fit in well with the Halloween aesthetic. You can line your driveway with them or make them the centerpiece in your room. These pinwheels require delicate cuts, so it is better to use thin paper instead of cardboard or hard materials.

For Halloween, you can also make banners out of felt. You can write 'Happy Halloween!', 'Halloween is Here!', or absolutely anything you like. These DIY-Halloween banners look regal and enticing placed or hung on the Halloween mantel. You can stick iron-on vinyl or glitter stickers on these to make them more appealing to your children. You can also design 'haunted' doormats with creepy drawings cut out on them or quotes written in a horror-inspired font. Bring all your ideas to the table! Everything is possible when you have a Cricut smart-cutting device. You can also make Halloween-inspired DIY-earrings for yourself or your loved ones! All you have to do is get hold of a rigid material and cut it into identical shapes. You can make pumpkins, ghosts, or spider-webs. You can also make a wreath out of the spider-webs you print and cut out using your Cricut machine. These look intricate and beautiful and will undoubtedly catch the eye of every visitor. They meld perfectly with other Halloween-themed designs. With your Cricut device, you can also make a signboard. You can also cut out a quote or label for it, using the Cricut machine you own.

You can also design and create DIY-plates for Halloween, with drawings and designs of skeletons on top of them. You can either cut and paste vinyl stickers or emboss shapes of a pumpkin on the plates. You can decorate mason jars filled with candy for the children and make witch hats with paper for their metallic lids. You can also make a paper candy box in the shape of a haunted house with a Cricut and some well-placed glue. To entertain the children, you can print and cut out coloring books using your Cricut machine. You can design a garland with small cut out pieces of paper shaped like candy corn. Fill in the colors for a fun activity with your kids, and hang it anywhere you like. Halloween is a great time for celebration, art, and design! You can also make customized candy wraps and design blank tote bags with Halloween-themed drawings and patterns.

A few other things that you can make with a Cricut machine are as follows:

- **Stickers**

  You can make a variety of stickers of all types using a simple Cricut machine. These include 3-D stickers that can be used for laptops, car dashboards, and to decorate your desk. You can also cut out stickers used for notebooks and journals, making taking notes and journaling so much more fun! As the market for laptop stickers is increasing, you can even start up your own small business where you sell customized stickers of your customers' choice. It's an easy and fun way to earn more money and spend your time learning new things.

- **Greeting cards**

Make professional-looking greeting cards with your very own Cricut. You can design and create cards for birthdays, anniversaries, and other holidays and events. Not only do they look relatively high-end, but they will also be hand-made, which makes whoever you give them to love them all the more!

- **3-D projects**

You can use your Cricut device to make gift boxes, paper toys, and wood items. Making 3-D art has never been more convenient! If you are a professional designer or an architect, you already the importance of making 3-D models and art. With a Cricut, you can construct these projects within minutes.

- **Clothing Items**

One of the easiest ways to cut clothes and fabric is with the help of a Cricut machine. You can also spice up your blank tees and Jeans with patches of vinyl or other fabric.

What Can't a Cricut Machine Do?

Some of the things that a Cricut *can't* do, however, are print and laminate. Cricut machines are incredibly good investments if you are interested in arts and crafts, but before you make the purchase, you should look into what a Cricut is comprised of and what it is capable of. Cricut devices also cannot sew clothing or fabric.

While Cricuts can cut all sorts of fabrics and cloth with ease, they certainly cannot sew them together. You will have to either buy a sewing machine or do it manually for your sewing and quilting projects. An excellent benefit of cutting fabric with a Cricut machine is that you can do it without a backing material. Backing materials are used to stabilize the cloth that you are cutting. A Cricut machine excels at accuracy and precision, and so a backing material is unnecessary.

Chapter 3: Types of Cricut Machines

So far, we have learned what Cricut machines are and how they are used to spice up your home décor and life. But how do you know which Cricut device is ideal for you? Like smartphones and other electronic items, the Cricut smart-cutting machine comes in several variants and models. Each one has different abilities and specs, making it perfect for just the right kind of user. All users have different needs– and so, the other Cricut machine models are tailored to cater to the corresponding user's needs. They are also differently priced, so before you purchase a Cricut machine, you must keep your needs, requirements, and budget in mind.

The learning curve of a Cricut machine is not that hard to master. It is a bit tricky at first to understand how to use it, and it can get overwhelming for someone who is not used to using electronic devices. But Cricuts were designed for people of all age groups and from all walks of life, so even though it might seem intimidating at first, with its confusing shape and build, it can get relatively easy-to-use and straightforward with just a little bit of practice.

There are many ways to learn how to use a Cricut device, namely, watching YouTube videos, reading the manual, looking for tutorials online, or reading this book. Living in the information age, everything is at the tip of your fingers. All you have to do is a simple Google search to know how to work a Cricut machine.Of course, the different Cricut models each need a different set of instructions to work. But what exactly are the types of Cricut machines out there? Read on to find out!

With the different Cricut machines raging in the markets these days, it can be unclear to know which one is the right machine for you. The ideal approach is to break down each Cricut device's capabilities and crafts before you decide on the model to buy. Different types of crafters may need different kinds of devices. It is because each machine is catered to a diverse audience. You might need a more specialized cutting tool if you are an expert, as opposed to if you are a beginner. Luckily, Cricut models are tailored towards pleasing all kinds of people. Whether you are a starter or a professional craftsperson, a Cricut device can certainly help you out either way.

Cricut has released several models over the years since the brand's launch. These were computer-controlled cutting devices designed for DIY-crafters or home-crafters, artists, and designers. Most of these machines could cut through stiff fabric, paper, and materials like felt and even wood. It spiked the popularity of the Cricut machines, as the market for smart-cutting tools, especially for beginners and starters, did not offer much.

Some of the devices that Cricut initially released have been discontinued over the years. In the discussion and description following this, we will talk about the current Cricut models and the legacy models. Their details and purposes are all worth taking a look at. Even though some of the models are outdatedand obsolete, you will still be able to buy them in machinery markets or online electronics shopping stores like Amazon. However, there is no use purchasing these as even though you may be able to buy them at low costs and brand new, they are still not used anywhere, and finding their components in case of accidents or damages is quite unlikely.

Why would you buy a machine when a newer, much more advanced version is already gracing the markets? The decision, however, is yours entirely. It would help if you made an educated decision based on all the facts and knowledge you acquire. Reading this chapter (and this book) can undoubtedly assist you in making the right decision.

Legacy Models

The legacy models are outdated, obsolete ones that are not in circulation anymore. Although you might be able to get your hands on one of these at cheap rates, it is not recommended to buy them for various reasons and disadvantages. These include the original Cricut machine that offered mats of 6-by-12 inches only. The latest Cricuts have mats of 12-by-12 inches, so you can see why those would be preferable to the original ones. Another discontinued variant of the Cricut brand is the Cricut Cake. The Cricut Cake was used to cut out edible fondants into shapes of any kind out of fondant sheets. Chefs and cooks mostly used this to prepare and decorate all sorts of cakes. It was indeed a creative venture by the Cricut machines.

The Original Cricut

The Original Cricut was used to cut images in a height range of 1-inch to 5-and-a-half inches. This version of the Cricut was compatible with all original cartridges that Cricut made. This machine's drawback is that it can't cut as diverse a range of products and materials that the newer Cricuts can. Cricut did release, however, a Deep Cut Blade and Housing that allows owners of the Original Cricut to cut materials that are 1.55 mm thick, including magnets, stamp materials, and chipboard. This Cricut is also compatible with the Cricut Design Craft Room.

The Cricut Imagine

The Cricut Imagine was unique in the sense that it had an in-built HP-97 inkjet printer. It allowed the device to both print and cut out images and patterns. Although this device only lasted one year, it had some great qualities. It had a remodeled touch screen interface. The one drawback of the Cricut Imagine is that it was quite large and hefty. Carrying it wasn't very enjoyable. Maybe that is why it was discontinued and is now rarely found.

The Cricut Expression

The Cricut Expression was a considerable upgrade from the Original Cricut. It is because it had several advantages over the previous device. It came with a 12-by-12 inch cutting mat and allowed users to cut shapes and fonts from 0.25-inches up to 23-

and-a-half inches. It had adjustable slides, so users did not have to trim their media down to 6-by-12 inches before cutting. The Cricut Expression could also cut a broader range of materials than the Original Cricut machine could. These materials included vellum, vinyl, chipboard, thin foils, and fabrics. THIS Cricut model also hosted an LCD Screen that could be used to preview the work. It had features like Quantity and Auto-Fill. You could choose a 'Paper Saver' mode, and a choice of Landscape or Portrait mode was also added to this model. The standard Cricut Expression included two cartridges that came with the device, a Plantin SchoolBook and Accent Essentials.

The Cricut Expression 2

The updated model of the Cricut Expression had a revamped exterior. It also came with a 12-by-12 inch mat used for cutting. The keyboard that the Original Cricut and the Cricut Expression had was not featured in this model of the Cricut. In its place, the Cricut Expression 2 features a brand new full-color LCD touch-screen. The LCD touch-screen had a keyboard on the screen that could be used to see where the images will be on the mat before beginning the cutting process. This model also features a new, independent image-sizing and image-rotation function in the LCD Screen that was missing from previous models.

The Cricut Mini

Unlike the other Cricuts, the Cricut Mini is a small and mini-sized cutting machine designed for personal use. This Cricut only worked with a computer as it could not cut images standalone.

You had to use the Cricut Craft Room design software to use this Cricut machine. The Cricut Mini came with over 500 images that were automatically unlocked as you connected your Cricut to the Cricut Room software. This model featured a cartridge port compatible with the Cricut cartridges, excluding the Cricut Imagine cartridges. It also had a unique mat size of 8.5-by-12 inches. The size range that this Cricut could cut images in was 0.24 inches to 11-and-a-half inches. It would be useless buying this device now as the Cricut Mini relied heavily on the Craft Room design software, which is not functioning any longer. Out of all the other Cricut legacy devices, the Cricut Mini is the only one that is obsolete and unusable in any way.

The Cricut Cake

The Cricut Cake was one of the first cutters that could cut vinyl. You could cut edible vinyl with this remarkable device. The Cricut Cake was only designed for cakes, as you could tell by the name itself. You could still cut vinyl and iron-on materials with this model of the Cricut machine, though. Today, it would not be ideal to buy the Cricut Cake except for cooking purposes as the newer models of the Cricut offer much more to the users than this one.

Current Models

Unlike the Legacy models of the Cricut that are no longer sold or supported by Cricut, the current models are sold and supported by the Cricut brand. There are three current models of the Cricut:

- The Cricut Maker
- The Cricut Joy
- The Cricut Explore Air 2

The previous models in the Cricut Explore family, the Cricut Explore Air, the Cricut Explore, and the Cricut Explore One were discontinued but are still supported by Cricut. They are compatible with the Design Space software. The Cricut Cuttlebug, another Cricut model that was used for die-cutting and embossing, was also discontinued in the spring of 2019.

The Cricut Joy

The Cricut Joy is the newest Cricut machine released in February 2020. It is a smaller and more lightweight version of the Cricut machine, aimed at casual crafters. This teeny-tiny device can be used to cut and draw on a wide variety of materials, including vinyl and iron-on, even without a mat. The Cricut Joy is a compact little device that is half the Cricut Explore and the Cricut Maker's size, which makes it quite portable and easy to carry. It comes with a single blade and pen holder, and its cut width is 4.5 inches. The Cricut Joy introduced two brand new features: the ability to cut materials without a mat and cutting up to four feet long designs in a single go! The Cricut Joy also came with a Card

Mat, which allowed the user to make cards for all occasions. You could also make repeated cuts up to 20 feet long with the Cricut Joy.

The Cricut Maker

The Cricut Makers is for the serious crafters. Introduced in the August of the year 2017, the Cricut Maker is ten times more powerful than the Explore Air 2, despite being somewhat similar in looks and design. The Cricut Maker can cut, draw, emboss, deboss, score, and more! This device is a must-have if you are a professional designer or craftsperson.

The Cricut Maker was designed to cut thicker and sturdier materials, like balsa wood, basswood, leather, felt, and non-bonded fabric. This device can do everything that the Explore family of Cricuts can do, but with added features. This top-of-the-line cutting machine can cut non-bonded fabric without a stabilizer, unlike the Cricut Explore line, using only a tiny Rotary Blade. The Cricut Maker is the only Cricut machine that supports the use of this Rotary Blade, which cuts beautifully and with high precision. Materials like felt and fabric can be cut quite easily with the Maker, so if you are a fabric or felt craftsperson, the Cricut Maker is the perfect device for you. The Cricut Maker also supports a single Scoring Wheel or double Scoring Wheel that can apply varied pressure to score thicker materials than the original Scoring Stylus that used the QuickSwap housing. The Cricut Maker can achieve all sorts of materials with this Scoring Wheel.

In the July of 2019, some new tools were announced for the Cricut Maker. These are as follows:

- The Perforation Blade
- The Engraving Tip
- The Wavy Rotary Blade
- The Debossing Tip

This expansive adaptive tool system was designed with the advancement in mind. It can be used to build all sorts of things and items. Although the Cricut Maker is slightly on the pricey side, it is still quite worth it, especially if you are a professional artist or designer. Even sewing experts and fans, paper-crafters, and woodworkers would do well to buy this smart-cuttingmachine.

The Cricut Explore family

The Cricut Explore family can cut through the same materials, but each model in this line has slightly different features. The Cricut Explore One and Explore Air had much of the same characteristics. The prior had a single tool holder, whereas the latter sported two tool holders as well as a Bluetooth connection. Although Cricut no longer sells these devices, you can buy them used on Amazon.

The Cricut Explore Air 2 is a new addition to the Explore line of Cricut devices. It has three additional colors: Mint Blue, Rose Anna, and Giffin Lilac. This model also features a Fast Mode, which offers two times faster cutting of materials like vinyl, iron-on heat transfer vinyl, and cardboard. The Cricut Explore Air 2 is cheaper than the Cricut Maker and is almost always on sale so that users can buy it on a budget. The high-powered cutting machine can cut through faux leather, suede, felt, and over a hundred other materials. It is a fantastic machine for most users, and its various colors and sleek design make it all the moretempting to buy.

The Cricut Explore Air is a step down from the Cricut Explore Air 2 and is no longer sold by the Cricut brand. Thankfully, you can still buy it used or from other electronics retail stores. It is still compatible with the Design Space application. This model is Bluetooth-enabled, so it does not require the user to plug it in anywhere. It also features a secondary tool holder so you can hold several tools at once. You can write and cut, or score and cut, at the same time with the Explore Air.

The Cricut Explore One is also no longer available in Cricut stores. It is the standard Cricut Explore device, which is also quite economical and reasonable-priced. It offers accurate and precise cutting, writing, as well as scoring. You can cut several materials with the Cricut Explore One. However, it is not Bluetooth-enabled, so you do need to connect it to your computer with a plug or cord. You also can't write and cut or score and cut at the same time with the Cricut Explore One.

Chapter 4: How to Set Up a Cricut Machine?

Before you buy your Cricut device, it is best to be fully prepared for what to expect. It is not easy to set up a machine you know nothing about, and Cricuts, like all electronic devices, are complicated to get started. Don't worry, though– once you get the hang of it, it becomes significantly easier. The different Cricut models all come with different items and materials and have diverse specialties. It's much easier to understand how to work these machines once we know this.

The Cricut models are the Cricut Joy, the Cricut Maker, and the Cricut Explore Air 2. Although all are capable and advanced smart-cutting tools, they come at different price ranges and have other special skills.

The Cricut Joy

The Cricut Joy comes with the following additional materials:

- Blade and Housing
- Fine Point Pen
- StandardGrip Mat
- Deluxe Paper or Adhesive-Backed Deluxe Paper
- Smart Vinyl

The Cricut Joy coming with so many new materials and additional features makes it a mighty and high-demand cutting machine. Let's take a more in-depth look at these components of the Cricut Joy.

Blade and Housing

The Blade that comes with the Cricut Joy is recommended to cut popular materials like iron-on, vinyl, and paper. These can be used to make home décor, decals, and even hand-made cards. The Cricut Joy Blade can also be used with popular DIY materials like cardstock, poster boards, and others. These blades are also compatible with exclusively Cricut Joy materials, including Infusible Ink Transfer Sheets, Insert Cards, and Smart Materials. There is a full list of all the materials that the Cricut Joy is compatible with on the Cricut website. The Cricut Joy Blade Housing is in silver and white colors. It looks quite sleek and regal. The Cricut Joy Blade is only compatible with the Cricut Joy Machine and the Cricut Joy Blade Housing. The Blade will not work with the Cricut Maker or the Cricut Explore Air.

The Cricut Joy Blades are designed to provide precise cutting and durability. However, just like other electronic items and blades, with use and the passage of time, the Cricut Joy Blades will also dull with use and require replacements.

To replace a Cricut Joy Blade, you have to take the following steps:

1. First, open the clamp and pull, in a straight manner, the Blade Housing to remove it.

2. Secondly, push the button on top of the Blade Housing and then very carefully and cautiously remove the Cricut Joy Blade.

3. Take hold of the new Cricut Joy Blade and remove the clear protective capping.

4. Insert this new Blade into the Blade Housing from the conical side. Do not put the cutting end into the Blade Housing. This may damage both the new Cricut Joy Blade and the Blade Housing. A magnet is present that will hold the Blade in place.

5. Place the Blade Housing back into the clamp of the Cricut Joy.

Once the Blade Housing is merged with the top of the clamp, close it.

Fine Point Pen

The Fine Point Pen is used to decorate your projects with a personal touch using your Cricut Joy Machine. You might have the question of how to install pens and markers into your Cricut Joy. It might seem not very clear, but it is relatively easy. Design Space will automatically alert you when the time comes to insert your pen or marker. The steps to be taken to insert a Fine Point Pen are as follows:

1. Initially, you must open the clamp.

2. Secondly, you remove the Blade Housing and put it aside in a safe place, away from the reach of children orpets.

3. Remove the capping from the Cricut Joy Fine PointPen.

4. Place the Fine Point Pen inside the clamp and allow it to fix into place. Drop it. There is no need to press or wait for it to click.

5. Close the clamp carefully.

And that's it! Your Cricut Joy is ready to draw with the wondrous and exquisite Fine Point Pen!

StandardGrip Mat

The StandardGrip Mat is a reusable adhesive mat that secures the materials needed for cutting and writing. Cricut Joy can cut out Smart Materials even without using a machine mat, but it can use the machine mat to cut a few other things. Machine mats have adhesive on an area that provides just the right grip to hold your material in place. If you are working with paper or fabric, this can be quite helpful. With the Cricut Joy, you can use three different mats: the LightGrip Mat, the StandardGrip Mat, and the Card Mat.

The Card Mat is designed exclusively with a divider, the sole purpose of which is to protect the back of the folded Cricut Insert Cards as you cut a design on the front. The LightGrip Mat comes in a 4.5-by-12 inch size and is perfect for cutting light-medium weight papers, as well as medium cardstock and materials like vinyl.

The StandadGrip Mat is available in a 4.5-by-6.5 inch and 4.5-by-12 inch size. It is excellent for cutting vinyl, iron-on, poster boards, and heavy cardstock. This mat can also be used to cut Smart Material scraps that are too small to be cut without a mat.

What Can You Cut with a Cricut Joy?

Cricut Joy machines can cut through a range of standard materials. Some of the materials it can cut through are noted down below. The cut settings for these materials can already be found in Design Space.

- Flat Cardboard
- Foil Poster Cardboard
- Corrugated Cardboard
- Insert Card Cardstock
- Glitter Cardstock
- Medium Cardstock
- Paper-thin Faux Leather
- Deluxe Paper
- Adhesive-backed Deluxe Paper
- Shimmer Paper
- Sparkle Paper
- Smart Label Writable Paper
- Foil Paper
- True Brushed Paper

- Pearl Paper
- Foil Acetate
- Holographic Iron-On
- Smart Iron-On
- Everyday Iron-On
- Glitter-Mesh Iron-On
- Premium Vinyl
- Holographic Vinyl
- Chalkboard Vinyl
- Dry Erase Vinyl
- Smart Vinyl
- Stencil Vinyl
- Window Cling
- Party Foil
- And many more

Smart Materials

The Cricut Joy comes with a few Smart Materials. No cutting mat is needed for these Smart Materials. These crafting materials can just be loaded directly into your Cricut Joy machine. There are many Smart Materials that Cricut creates, but the one you get as an addition to the Cricut Joy is Smart Vinyl. The other Smart Materials include Smart Iron-On, Smart Label Writable Vinyl, and Smart Label Writable Paper.

Using Smart Materials is helpful because Cricut Joy machines can cut a shape continuously that is 4 feet long and 4.5 inches wide! It can also make repeated cuts, such as shapes like hearts or stars, for up to 20 feet. This is a legendary feat that the Cricut Joy is capable of with Smart Materials. With other materials, the size of your cutting mat will limit your design size.

With Smart Materials, Cricut Joy can cut an individual, continuous shape up to 4.5 inches wide and 4 feet long, and make repeated cuts (like stars, hearts, and confetti) up to 20 feet long! For all other materials, the size of your mat would limit the size of your design.

How to Connect Your Cricut Joy with Bluetooth?
The Cricut Joy makes use of Bluetooth tech to connect to your device, be it iOS, Android, or even Bluetooth-enabled Windows or Mac computers. Follow the steps detailed below to secure your Windows device via Bluetooth.

1. Plug your Cricut Joy in and turn the power on.

2. Ensure that the Cricut Joy is near to your computer, approximately 10 to 15 feet away.

3. To determine that your computer is Bluetooth-enabled, right-click on the Start button and select Device Manager.

4. If you find Bluetooth listed, it means that your computer is Bluetooth-enabled. If it is not, you will need to purchase a USB device known as a Bluetooth Dongle, which will enable your computer to connect via Bluetooth to other devices.

5. Close the Device Manager. Go to the Settings of your computer. You will find a section titled 'Bluetooth and Other Devices.' Click on this.

6. Ensure that the Bluetooth option is turned on, and click on 'Add Bluetooth or other device'.

7. Wait for your computer to recognize and detect the Cricut Joy machine. Select the Cricut Joy Bluetooth module name from the list of Bluetooth devices available for connection to initiate the pairing. If you are unsure of your Cricut device's name, it can be found on the bottom of the machine. Just turn it over and find out.

8. Your Cricut device is now connected via Bluetooth!

Similarly, if you want to connect your Cricut Joy via Bluetooth to a Mac computer, the steps would be as follows:

1. Ensure that your Cricut Joy and computer are powered on. Make sure your Cricut Joy is within 10 to 15 feet of the computer.

2. Mac computers are usually Bluetooth-enabled, but you can open Apple Menu and click on System Preference to check. Look for the Bluetooth option here.

3. Click on the Bluetooth window. If Bluetooth is turned off, you can click the button to turn it on. Find the name of your Cricut Joy module in the list of devices available.

Then click on Pair or Connect to connect your device via Bluetooth.

4. There you go! Your cutting machine is connected to your Mac computer.

For an Android phone or device, the steps are slightly altered. You will need to follow the steps below to connect your Cricut Joy to an Android device with Bluetooth.

1. The same as before, keep your Cricut machine within 10 to 15 feet of distance of the Android device.

2. Open Settings in your Android device or phone and click on Bluetooth.

3. Ensure that Bluetooth is turned on.

4. Select the name of the Cricut Joy module in the list of available devices on your phone. Tap on it to initiate pairing.

5. Your Cricut Joy is now connected to your Android device!

The steps to connect via Bluetooth to an iOS device are slightly different. Many people worldwide use Apple phones, and securing your Cricut Joy device to your iPhone or iPad will make the design process much more straightforward. The steps to connect your Apple device to the Cricut Joy are:

1. Keep your Cricut Joy near the iOS device.

2. Click on Settings and then Bluetooth.

3. Tap to turn Bluetooth on if it is turned off.

4. Select your Cricut device's module name on the list of available devices present to initiate the pairing.

5. Cricut Joy is now paired with the iOS device you own!

Please note that the Cricut Joy module name is found on the bottom of the Cricut Joy machine.

The Cricut Maker

The Cricut Maker comes with the following items:

- Rotary Blade and Drive Housing
- Premium Fine Point Blade and Housing
- Fine Point Pen
- FabricGrip Machine Mat
- LightGrip Mat
- Cardstock and Fabric

The Rotary Blade cuts through most fabrics smoothly, almost gliding through the delicate materials without the need for a backing material. The Premium Fine Point Blade seamlessly flows through light to medium weight paper and materials like iron-on, vinyl, and cardstock. Embellishing your crafts with beautiful texts and hand-drawn shapes is the Fine Point Pen. A FabricGrip Mat, which is easy-release and reusable, is used to cut fabric and fabric-bonded materials. The LightGrip machine mat is also reusable and soft-release and is used to cut light or medium-weight materials. The Cricut Maker comes with cardstock and fabric to get you started on your first sample project. Remember– practice is everything!

Just like the Cricut Joy, the Cricut Maker can also be connected to your computer or phone via Bluetooth. The steps followed are the same, so go on above and read them to get started.

The Cricut Explore Air 2

Included with the Cricut Explore Air 2 are a Welcome Book, a power adapter, and a USB cable. The other items you get along with a Cricut Explore Air 2 are:

- Premium Fine-Point Blade and Housing
- Fine Point Pen
- LightGrip Machine Mat
- Cardstock

These materials are provided for the same reason they are supplied with the Cricut Maker and the Cricut Joy; to help you get started and ease your transition from a designer to a professional smart-cutting tool user.

How to Set Up Your Cricut Device?

Setting up your Cricut device will automatically register your account with the machine. To set up your Cricut device, follow the steps written below. Note that these steps will only work for Windows and Mac computers. The steps for Android devices and iOS ones are slightly different and will be detailed later on in this chapter. Keep reading to find out!

1. Plugin your Cricut smart-cutting machine and turn the power on.

2. Use a USB cord or Bluetooth to connect the machine to your computer or laptop. The steps for how to connect via Bluetooth were mentioned previously.

3. Open the following link on your computer's browser: design.cricut.com/setup.

4. Download and then install the software Design Space for Desktop.

5. Follow the instructions that are given to you by the application and create your Cricut ID. Set up your new machine with this ID.

6. When the set-up is complete, you will be asked to do a test cut.

For Android and iOS devices, the process is similar but slightly altered. For your ease and convenience, we have written the steps down below.

1. Plugin your Cricut smart-cutting machine and turn the power on.

2. Turn Bluetooth on your iOS or Android device and pair the Cricut device by clicking or tapping on the Cricut module's name.

3. Download the Design Space App for Android and iOS, and then install it.

4. Launch the app once it has finished installing. Sign in with your account details or create a new Cricut ID.

5. Locate the menu in the Design Space App and then select Machine Setup.

6. Select the model of your Cricut device and then follow the on-screen instructions to complete the set-upprocess.

When you are prompted to do a test cut, you will know that the set-up is completed.

Chapter 5: How to Use a Cricut Machine?

Using a Cricut machine isn't easy if you have no prior instructions. But once you get the hang of it, you'll be able to cut and score patterns and images in no time! Installing Design Space is crucial to working with a Cricut. We already learned how to pair our Cricuts with our smartphones and computer devices in the last chapter, but how do we work with Design Space? This chapter covers that and much more.

In the previous years, Cricut used to have an online version, but now once you have installed the software, you can use it offline. That feature is, up until now, only valid for iOS and Windows. To use Design Space on Android, you need to have a stable Internet connection. When connecting and setting up your device, there are three essential steps you must take. The first of them is downloading, installing, and setting up the Design Space software. To use a Cricut machine, it must have a grasp on the Design Space App. Luckily the interface of the software is user-friendly and easy-to-learn. It is quite simple to use, and you will love it!

Are you enjoying the book? If so, I'd be happy if you could write a short review on Amazon. It would mean a lot to me. Thank you.

Installing Design Space

Installing the Design Space App on Windows, iOS, or Android is relatively easy. For Android and Apple, the Design Space App is available on both Google Play and App Store, respectively, by the name 'Cricut Design Space'. If you are on a Windows laptop or computer, all you need to do is open your browser and launch the following website:

https://design.cricut.com/#/launcher

Click on download to download the file. Once fully finished, click on the downloaded app in the Downloads folder or at the bottom of the web browser's window. A pop-up prompt will ask you if you wish to install. Once you agree, the app will be installed. The Cricut Design Space App will open up once the installation is complete. It is a small window with the Cricut logo and a login page. Before you start to use your Cricut machine, you need to connect it to the Design Space software.

With a MacBook, the process is similar. You go to the Cricut website and download the software, and then start the installation process. When opened, a small window with the Cricut logo will appear, along with an Applications icon. Click on the Cricut logo and drag it into the Applications icon. Once you do this, the Applications folder will open up. Click on the Cricut Design Space App. A warning prompt will appear. If you have downloaded the Design Space App from the authentic Cricut website, it is okay to go ahead. However, if you have installed the app from a third-party website or launcher, you should think again. Installing from suspicious websites can lead to malware and cyber-security threats attacking your device. It is recommended only to install Design Space from the original Cricut website. Once the Cricut Design Space App is open, you will be asked to enter your details and log in.

The Design Space installation process for iPhones and iPads requires opening up the main Apple store for App Store applications and games. You must search for 'Cricut Design Space', but even searching for 'Design Space' or 'Cricut' can lead you to the official app. Tap the small-sized cloud icon to install the app and open it once done. You will be asked to log in. you must connect and set up the Cricut machine before moving on and using Cricut.

For Android smartphones and tablets, you must open Google Play Store and search for the app. Once downloaded, enter your login details and connect to the Cricut smart-cutting machine by keeping it within 15 feet of the device.

Signing Up for Design Space

Once you are done with the installation process, you need to log in before using your Cricut machine. No matter which operating system or device you are using with your Cricut, the process is quite similar. Click on the green 'Machine Setup' button. When the Cricut Setup window opens, choose the Cricut machine you own that you want to pair with. The options are Cricut Maker, Cricut Explore Family, Cricut Joy, and Cricut EasyPress 2. The

EasyPress option is not available on Android or iOS devices. Before choosing your Cricut machine, you should already have connected it to the machine either via Bluetooth or with acable.

Fill in the information needed to create a new Cricut ID. This will register your account and give you all the details necessary to log in. You will have signed up and have now been a part of the Cricut Design Space software. If you already have an ID, click on 'Sign In' and enter your details. With this ID, you have the option of logging in via other devices too, and you can also log in to the Cricut website and make new purchases, such as blades, pens, and markers.

Once you are on the 'Get Connected' window, Cricut will tell you how to connect your device. Your Cricut machine should appear connected, as you have already secured the device before.

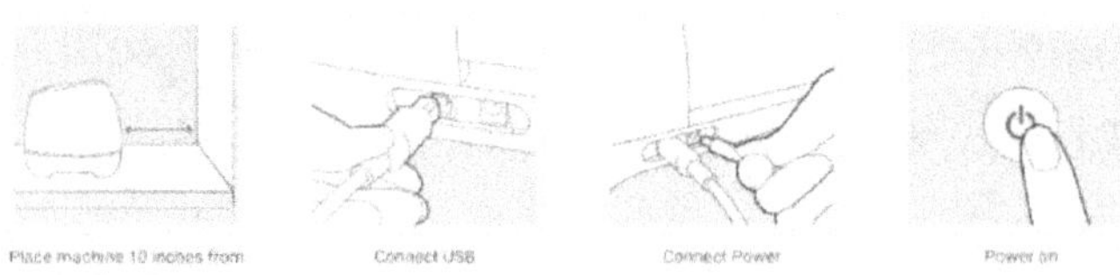

Testing a Cut

When you click on 'Continue,' you will be led to a window that says 'Let's Test a Cut.' Testing a cut is quite simple. Cricut asks you to choose an image from the following list of shots. You click on the one you want to cut as a test. Cricut will also give you the instructions needed to make the very first cut. If you are already aware of how to cut with a Cricut, you can click on 'Skip'.

Testing a cut is important because materials come in different thicknesses and all Cricut machines cut them differently. You don't want to be in for any surprises before you make the final cut. Pick a few simple shapes to cut at first for your test cut. On the Design Space app, insert a square and then a triangle right atop it. Resize the triangle, so it fits inside the middle of the square. This will give you a few different directions that the blade will cut in.

Apply 'Select All' by right-clicking or pressing the keyboard shortcut, CTRL + A, to select everything. Keep the two images together. You don't need too big of a cut size, so you can change the size to whatever you think is appropriate, and voila! Everything is good to go. Once this is done, send the design over to your machine to cut. This test cut won't use a lot of your material, so don't worry about wasting any vinyl or fabric. Press 'Continue'. This will send it over to your machine to cut.

There you go! Your machine is ready to cut. Just load the vinyl and press the 'Go' button. It will cut at the top-left corner of the vinyl. Make sure that your machine's settings are set to vinyl, so it cuts precisely and accurately.

Once your pattern or image is cut, unload the vinyl from the machine. You can pick up the small cut-out square. If the triangle has stayed in its place, the image or pattern will have cut out perfectly. If not, adjust and readjust the settings to your liking and preferences, and try cutting once more. Test cuts help you decide the right settings for all the different kinds of materials.

Print-Then-Cut   Calibration

What is Print-Then-Cut calibration? If you haven't heard of it before, don't worry! This is quite a simple function of some of the Cricut devices. Print-Then-Cut ensures that your Cricut machine can cut along the edges and outlines of your images accurately and precisely. The steps to calibrate with a Windows device and an iOS device are different. Calibration is not available on Android devices, at the moment.

For Windows and MacOS Devices

The steps to calibrate Windows and MacOS devices are as follows:

1. Open Design Space and sign in.

2. Select the account menu and click on 'Calibration.'

3. Choose the 'Print Then Cut' option.

4. Select the printer you are using, which is connected to your PC, and then click on 'Print.'

5. Put the calibration sheet that you have printed on the machine's cutting mat. Position it on the top-left of the mat. Click on 'Continue.'

6. Ensure that your Cricut device is powered ON. It should also be connected to the computer or laptop via Bluetooth or a USB cable.

7. On the following screen, select your Cricut type from the drop-down menu.

8. Select the right material setting, load the cutting matinto the machine, and press 'Go.'

9. Your Cricut device will begin the scan for the sheet of calibration markings. Once it has scanned properly, it will cut around the small square centering the sheet.

10. Do not unload the mat. Look at the cut and check if it touches the printed line all the way. If it does, click on 'Yes' in Design Space and move on over to the next step. If you select 'No,' the next step Design Space takes it to cut a little closer to the line. Once that is done, you will be able to fine-tune your calibration.

11. The Cricut machine will begin the calibration along the top and the side. Once finished, without unloading the cutting mat, take a closer look at the line along the top and

side. Design Space will ask you which number and letter cuts are closes to the lines. Click on the 'Top' and, once you are done, click on 'Continue.'

12. A confirmation cut will be performed by the Cricut, which will be a large rectangle. When you are done experimenting with your Cricut, unload the mat, remove the calibration sheet, and carry on.

13. If you are pleased with the cut, click on 'Yes' and then 'Continue' to finish the calibration process. You will proceed to the final calibration screen.

14. If you select 'No,' you will have to refine and retune the calibration process.

15. Sometimes more than one calibration is necessary. Save and Close your calibration settings.

There you go! You are ready to Print-Then-Cut!

For iOS Devices

Now that we have learned how to apply Print-Then-Cut calibration on Windows and MacOS devices, we will look at how to calibrate iOS devices: iPhones and iPads. Before you do this, make sure that your device is connected to your Cricut machine via Bluetooth pairing. This is quite simple and is described in the previous chapters in detail.

1. Open the Cricut Design Space iOS application. Tap on the account menu.

2. Click on 'Print Then Cut Calibration.' A new window will appear.

3. Print out the sheet for calibration on your printer. Select 'Print Sheet' on the screen, which is present on the bottom right.

4. A preview of the calibration sheet will be shown next. If the printer you are connected to isn't appearing, click on the option' Select Printer'. From the list of options available, select your home printer.

5. Return to 'Printer Options' and select 'Print,' an option present on the screen's upper-right side. The calibration will be printed out.

6. Place this freshly-printed sheet on the machine mat, and adjust its position until it is on the top-left side of the mat. Select 'Continue'.

7. Select the right material setting. Load the mat onto the machine and press the 'Go' button.

8. The machine will scan the calibration sheet for the markings. It will proceed to cut around the square, first.

9. Before unloading the mat, check if the cut is accurate. If it is, tap on 'Yes' in Design Space on your iOS device. Then click on 'Continue.'

10. The Cricut will begin cutting on the calibration along the top and side of the sheet. Once it is finished, before you

unload the mat, look at the lines it has cut. If they seem even and accurate, tap on 'Continue.'

11. Once the confirmation cut is complete and looks impeccable and perfect, you can unload the cutting mat and remove the calibration sheet. If you are satisfied with the cut, tap on 'Yes' and then on 'Done' to save the calibration settings and return to the main Home screen.

12. You are ready to Print-Then-Cut!

This is all there is to know how to use the Cricut machine and the Design Space application. However, there is a lot more to know about the Design Space App, and its numerous features and functions. Read on to find out!

Chapter 6: The Different Materials that Cricut can Cut

The Cricut machine is often used as an excellent option for those who like to create beautiful pictures on their own or as a gift for someone special. Many people may have asked what the different materials that a Cricut Machine can cut through. One of the most important things to consider about a Cricut machine is what kind of material the cutting blade will be made from. Some devices can even cut glass, paper, and plastic. These are all types of materials that will look great in a picture. Of course, some may prefer a more natural-looking product.

Some people like to use wood, and some will use metal. There are even people who like to use other kinds of substances, but they will want to know what these materials are. Another significant factor to consider is the thickness of the paper. Some people may not want a thick cut because it will seem odd. Other people may prefer a thicker piece of paper.

If you are using wood, you need to be sure that the wood is adequately treated before using a Cricut machine. Wood that is not treated correctly could cause a problem if it were to become wet while the paper would be dry. If you want to have the piece of paper cut to look like a real photograph or picture, you may have to sand it before you start the project. The idea is to make sure that it is smooth without any bumps or scratches. This way, you can get a good, close-cut that looks good and is smooth.

Once the paper has been sanded, the next step is to attach it to the Cricut machine's backing. Make sure that you do this carefully because it can be easily done wrong. You want to make sure that there are no gaps between the two pieces of paper or between the paper and the backing to look good when finished. Once the paper has been attached to the Cricut machine, you will have to press it to the frame or surface that you are cutting on. Make sure that you take your time in doing this and that it does not happen too quickly.

You may also want to try using another type of paper to help with making the cut. For instance, if you were to use graphite paper, it would make the cut a lot easier. Once you are satisfied that the paper is set in place, you can then start to cut it with the machine. It is essential to be careful here because cutting your paper too fast can cause mistakes.

You should make sure that the paper fits right when you are cutting it with the Cricut machine. Sometimes, a piece of paper can be cut very close to where it should not be, so you need to make sure that it is all set in place and is evenly spaced out. You will also want to make sure that you are not holding the paper too tight. This can cause problems, so you may want to make sure that you are using a little room to make sure that it is not too tight or loose. When you have finished cutting the paper, you can then glue it onto the circuit machine. You will want to make sure that you allow some space for the glue to dry before you press the paper into the machine.

What is Design Space and How to Use It?

Cricut has just announced a new online desktop version of its popular Cricut Design Studio. As of January 31, 2020, the new program will only be available on desktop computers, as previously, it was only available for laptop and mobile devices. It will still need an Internet connection to download or buy Cricut designs, but you can now use these designs right on your desktop computer from your desktop software of choice. The program works with the same basic interface that makes Cricut a popular desktop program and is compatible with Microsoft Office products such as Word, Excel, PowerPoint, and Outlook. To get started, you'll simply need to log in to the program's website, then choose the "Download" button from the main navigation bar.

From there, you'll need to select which design space you want to work with from the drop-down menus of different software packages. You should be able to choose from Photoshop Express, Photoshop Elements, or Corel Draw. Choose one that works best for you to save time while you are creating your new art. After downloading the program, you'll be able to start working on your first design in the program. A simple drag and drop feature allows you to move various files around within the project easily.

If you're looking for a quick way to learn how to create designs with Cricut Design Space, all you need to do is start from the first step to the last. You'll be able to add and edit different files within the design space with no trouble at all. Even if you don't have a lot of experience designing programs, it's easy to learn how to use these tools. If you know graphic design programs, you can still create some beautiful pieces using the software. You can even import your photo or sketchbooks into the design space, allowing you to create an original piece of artwork. Using this software can help you create some unique designs!

How to Perform Craft Cutting with Cricut

Cricut is one of the oldest and most well-known craft-cutting machines on the market. However, you may be wondering how to do craft cutting with the Cricut machine or try to find ways to create a Cricut masterpiece using your Cricut machine. Many Cricut enthusiasts who have been attempting their craft-cutting device for the first time have found that they have not successfully made a piece that is pleasing to the eye. The following is a guide to help you achieve a Cricut masterpiece's quality that will impress everyone present. To start with, you must know how to do the cut properly. To do this, you need to make sure that the paper is well trimmed before you start.

There is nothing worse than cutting your paper without trimming it correctly. After this step, you can move onto the next. The next thing you need to do is attach this material to the machine and then press it down to its cutting area. This step will ensure that you get the piece cut with accuracy, without too much movement on the paper. Once you have pressed the paper down firmly, you can now start working with it. You need to cut it accordingly so that it is even and flat. You need to remove all the excess paper to stay flat before you continue with the cut. When the piece has been cut, you need to cut the extra paper and then replace it into the tray where you used to keep it while you cut the rest of the paper.

Chapter 7: Design Space App

Downloading and installing Design Space App

It's easy to download and install the Cricut Design Space App, which allows you to design your picture or scrapbook from any desktop or laptop computer. You can create the design for your album in the software, choose the fonts and other features, and then save it to a local USB device. The free version of the program provides limited features like creating a background, color selection, and printing. If you would like to add photos or change the layout, you will have to purchase the program's fullversion.

This program is very user-friendly and easy to use to create a fun and creative project for your family and friends. It works with Windows or Mac operating systems. If you are thinking about downloading and installing the Cricut Design Space App, there are a few things to consider before doing so.

Downloading and installing the Cricut Design Space App will allow you to save your work to a local USB drive and print your artwork in a standard format. However, you will not be able to print in color or preview your finished project until you purchase the program's full version. If you don't want to spend money, you may wish to download the trial version and then decide if you would like to purchase the full version. It is a good idea because you can see how much work you need to create a professional-looking photo album. Many people prefer to download the trial version to see how much time and effort they need to put into their projects to ensure quality creation.

Once you have downloaded and installed the Cricut Design Space App, it is simple to use. You drag and drop your pictures and designs on your album page to create a unique scrapbook or album. You can choose from thousands of templates that you can easily find online. You may want to select a template with a photo to create an album with a personalized message or image that you took personally with the person you are making the scrapbook with.

Once you have downloaded and installed Cricut Design Space App, all you have to do is click on the "Add Scrapbook" button, and the software will automatically load a blank page where you can quickly and easily add photos and design space. On your scrapbook page. You can even use Cricut Design Space App as a tutorial tool by using the tutorial tools to teach your children the proper way to add text and image to a scrapbook.

Download and install Cricut Design Space App. You will never have to worry about outdated and obsolete software as it is always being updated to keep up with technological advances. If you download the free trial version, you can try it out first to determine whether it will be worth the cost. of the download.

Everything you need to know about Design Space Desktop App

If you have not yet gotten your hands on an All Things Cricut Design Space Desktop App, then you are missing out on the most popular way to create beautiful crafts and stickers. Cricut is quickly becoming one of the most popular ways to personalize your kids' craft projects, and they will love you forever for it. This program is perfect for a beginner in the craft and sticker world because it is designed for kids and grownups who enjoy Cricut. You can get started creating crafts in no time at all with the All Things Cricut Design Space Desktop App, and you will have a blast creating stickers, skills, and other things with your child's favorite characters on their desktops.

Many different things make Cricut so popular. The best thing about the Cricut design Space Desktop App is the fact that it gives you the ability to do a wide variety of different stickers and crafts right from your computer. Using this program, you will take any picture or clip art image and turn it into a sticker, skill, or sticker design. With this software, you will use the pen-like tools, stamps, and other toolbox tools to do different stickers and crafts. You will also be able to print out stickers and craft and design them to your liking. You will be able to upload these stickers into your computer through a USB cable and then print them out and glue them onto your desktop. It is the easiest way to do stickers and other crafts with Cricut.

Cricut Design Space Desktop App is also very user-friendly. The tutorials that come with it are easy to follow. If you want to do some Cricut crafts, then this is the program that you need to use. It is straightforward to use, and once you understand how to use it, you will wonder how you ever did anything without this fantastic program before. Make sure that you check out the All Things Cricut Design Space Desktop App if you want to learn more about making crafts with this unique Cricut design software.

Chapter 8: Problems You May Face with a Cricut and How to Solve Them

There are several problems you might face while using Cricut. If you have issues with this machine, here are some tips that will help you solve them. The first problem that you might encounter is a scratch on the surface of the Cricut machine. If you want to get rid of your problems with Cricut, you need to make sure that you are not scratching the device when you start using it. To do this, you should be sure to turn Cricut on.

You should make sure that the screws on Cricut are properly tightened. Once they are tightened, you should switch it off and put it away. You should then put a drop cloth over the machine's surface and let it stay on the device for a while. When you do this, the dust that is attached to the screws will be lifted away. You should then replace the wheels on Cricut. After you have done it, you can then turn the machine on. It will work fine afterthis.

When you are using Cricut, you should remember to wear gloves whenever working with this device. This is because the plastic used in the machine parts can scratch your hands if you are not careful. Also, you should never use your fingernails on the parts of Cricut. It is best to use your hand. When you are using this machine, you should also consider cleaning the parts. The following are some of the problems you might encounter when you clean the parts of Cricut.

The first thing you should do is remove the machine that you want to clean by removing the screw that goes into the machine.

Once you have removed it, you should clean the part with the dirt by using your fingernails. When you are cleaning the device, you should use a dry rag to wipe away the dirt and dust deposited onto the machine's parts. Once you have finished cleaning the machine, you should apply a few oil coats to the elements to prevent your device from cracking and breaking down.

Another problem that you may encounter while using the Cricut is that the ink cartridge has begun to deteriorate. To fix this problem, you should carefully take out the ink cartridge and replace it with a new one. After you have replaced it, you should start the machine again. However, you need to remember that you need to be careful because the ink cartridge is very sensitive to temperature fluctuations.

You should also make sure that you know how to change the battery for the Cricut. When the battery is low, you should stop using the machine and recharge it. You should never put the Cricut on a hot surface because the heat can cause the Cricut to break down and lose its parts. Instead, you should place it somewhere else where it will not be exposed to direct heat.

If you have any other problem using the Cricut, you should call your local Cricut dealer or manufacturer before buying a new one. There might be a better option available for you. When you are using this type of Cricut, you must take care of these simple problems to keep your machine running smoothly and not suffer any significant issues.

To avoid all of these problems, you should always practice acceptable maintenance practices while using the Cricut. One way you can do this is to have regular cleaning sessions on the Cricut. If you want to avoid getting into a Cricut machine breakdown, you should also ensure that it is well maintained. This way, your Cricut machine will work efficiently without experiencing breakdowns. It will help you get your projects completed in no time. To avoid breaking down your Cricut, you should never operate it at high temperatures and always store it in a cool, dryplace.

Chapter 9: Why Should You Invest in a Cricut?

When Cricut was first introduced, it was a great product to buy. It was a relatively cheap machine that offered many functions and was perfect for young children and their parents. To keep up with the times, the device has been updated and redesigned many times.

One of the features added to the machine that children's needs have demanded is a coloring screen. As we all know, kids love to color in pictures and drawings, and this feature makes it easy for them to do so. Another popular feature on the Cricut is the addition of an animated machine. In the past, these features were not included because they were too expensive to incorporate into the product.

Now, children are playing video games instead of coloring pictures, and they want to do both. The machine will automatically start when it senses the child moving around inside of the device. It then will move and rotate around the toy like a real Cricut machine would. You can also purchase additional accessories for your machine. These items are usually sold separately, and make life easier for parents, who have to buy them separately for their kids.

If you have a machine of this type that is not going to be used by your kids, you might want to consider giving it as a gift. Many people choose Cricut products because they are well made and designed and are great gifts that you can give out to family and friends. Next time you are looking to buy a Cricut, take a look at the many different available models. They are all great pieces of furniture for kids' rooms. If you can afford them, you may want to consider buying the one that comes with an animated machine or two!

Kids love playing with their Cricut machines, and they will find that it will be a lot more fun than going into a store and buying them some toys that are out of date and no longer have their favorite characters on them. You would be able to give them the Cricut toys that you would have chosen yourself if you had a Cricut machine of your own. When you are shopping for a Cricut machine, you will need to check the model number. Many times, it is on the bottom of the machine.

The best way to determine what model number is available is to find an expert who can help you in this search. They are going to be able to tell you which ones are still in production and which ones are no longer available. Then, you will need to do a little research to find the best value for your money. There are many different types of machines out there, so you should choose the ones that you think will give your kids the most enjoyment for the cost you are willing to pay.

Buying a Cricut machine is a significant investment, and you will enjoy it for many years to come. Your kids will love being able to create their artworks, and you will have a lot of happy memories that they can pass down from generation to generation! If you want to find out about the other Cricut machines available, you can also look online. Many stores specialize in this type of device, and they can provide you with much more information about the different available options.

Once you have decided how much you will spend on your new Cricut machine, you will need to determine how much you will spend on paper, ink, and all the other supplies that you will need to do the works. In most cases, you can get a good deal by buying a second-hand machine for the price of a brand new one, but there are always exceptions to this rule.

You will probably find that a Cricut machine can be a great way to make your child's room look much nicer than it looks when you buy a cheaper device, but if you are looking to make it look more like a real drawing, then you will probably be much better off spending the extra money on the more expensive Cricut machine. Make sure to keep this in mind as you shop. When you think about all the memories that you will be making when you make your first drawing, you will see that it is well worth it!

Chapter 10: Hacks that Every Cricut Beginner Should Know

The Cricut machine is one of the most well known and most loved craft items in the world. It is not that the device itself is a lousy piece of equipment or that people are not happy using it. Instead, it is the fact that the Cricut machine has several secrets that the beginner Cricut maker should know about to be success- ful at this craft.

Beginner Cricut makers should learn about the basic functions of each machine. They should become comfortable with inserting paper into the machine and what the various controls do. They should understand that the paper will come out of the device when the right combination of rollers and crayons is used. They should also know that the different colored paper comes out of the machine when the paper has been mixed properly. And they should understand that the paper will be folded and glued to make each piece.

If a Cricut machine beginner wishes to make an original piece, they should learn how to fill the machine up with all the supplies that are needed for the project. These supplies include paper, col- ors, crayons, and other supplies. Most beginner Cricut makers think that these supplies can be purchased from a store that sells crayons, but they are much more difficult to find than the sup- plies bought from an online store.

For those Cricut machine beginners that want to produce their first drawing, they should know that this process is also straight-forward. Once they have learned how to fill up the machine and draw, they should then learn how the crayons will go into the machine.

After they know how to use the machine to make their drawings, the Cricut machine beginner will need to learn how to draw and print their finished work. It is another area that beginners usually get confused when they start their own Cricut business. This is not to say that there is anything wrong with starting your own business, but many beginners get caught up in the idea of making a living off of crayons and end up trying to do everything themselves. Even though they can do this, they may not have the right skills to take their business to the next level.

A Cricut machine beginner should learn how to properly make their stickers and decals to have custom stickers and decals made for their customers. When people see their stickers and decals, they will have the ability to remember that they made for them. There are many ways that a Cricut machine beginner can learn about how to make custom stamps. They should be able to easily understand that they can purchase stencils online, get them in the mail, or get them made. When they have created enough stickers and decals, they should have the ability to make the labels themselves, but if they cannot find these resources, they should ask for help from their friends.

Finally, a Cricut machine beginner should understand that they can purchase a Cricut template and cut out unique shapes to cut out shapes they want to create independently. For example, if they're going to take a picture of a dog, they can get the image onto the machine, cut it out, place it on the paper, and then cut it out with a knife to make a heart.

This is an excellent way for Cricut machines to learn the basics of their business and learn about the different shapes that can be made on the machine. Once they understand that they can cut out shapes that they want to create, they should make some of their shapes and patterns that they can sell on their website or friends and family.

These are a few Cricut machine beginner hacks that every Cricut machine beginner should be familiar with before they ever start a business. By understanding all of these hacks, the Cricut machine beginner should be able to make sure that they understand how to use their machine and what kind of custom work they can do for their customers.

It takes time and effort to create a successful business, but many Cricut machine beginner hacks that every Cricut machine beginner should understand. Even if you have never made your Cricut products before, there are still hacks that every Cricut machine beginner should know of. It is really up to the Cricut beginner to learn these hacks and use them to their advantage.

Conclusions

First of all, think about the high cost of getting a Cricut machine. There are only two options. You can either buy a cheap version or buy an expensive one. The only reason you might not want to go this route is that the quality will be far less. Either way, you're going to spend more money than you should on a high-end Cricut machine.

Now, we get into the real question - why should you buy a Cricut machine? Why shouldn't you buy a more expensive machine instead? The answer lies in the fact that Cricut is still pretty much a cutting-edge product, and you have so many features available on today's devices that the high-priced versions don't compare. Here's why.

In my experience, the reason Cricut is so unique compared to other products is the fact that Cricut machines are made out of high-quality wood that has been cut and sanded by professional craftsmen. If you buy a less expensive device, chances are you're going to run into problems with the wood breaking down and the machine becoming unstable.

Another reason is that a Cricut machine is a machine designed to make high-quality art, not something that you want to use to make stickers. Sure, it's not going to give you the same quality as an expensive piece of art, but it's going to get the job done better. Another thing to consider when deciding to buy a Cricut machine is that they are trendy today. Not only that, but they are great investments as well. Cricut machines are very durable, and the machine's design means that you're not going to have to payout a ton of money to buy one. They do have some maintenance, which can be expensive, but it's well worth it.

Also, I would suggest that you don't buy a Cricut machine just because they look like a cheap version. that you can save a few dollars on. While a low-end Cricut machine may do a good job, they won't last long.

Instead, try to find a Cricut machine that will give you the quality you need, the design, and the durability to last you a while. If you buy a Cricut machine that is well built and durable, you should be able to afford to replace them much cheaper than if you choose a more affordable version.

So why should you buy a Cricut machine? Here are some reasons. First of all, the cost of buying a Cricut machine is much lower than buying a piece of art that you can print on your computer printer. With a good Cricut machine, you can print out thousands of stickers in a matter of minutes. With a less expensive machine, you're just going to print out a couple of stickers here and there.

This is a significant benefit of buying a Cricut machine because of the low cost of the product. Even if you buy a low-quality Cricut machine, you can buy more than enough of them to last you for years. And even if you buy a lower quality machine, you'll still be saving money.

One other reason to buy a Cricut machine is that they are incredibly versatile. You can use them in nearly any type of project. Whether you want to make posters, stickers, or you're interested in scrapbooking, you can easily create the designs you want with this fantastic product.

Also available from Paul S. Leland:

80

CRICUT PROJECT IDEAS

CRICUT DESIGN SPACE